Introduction

Wester Ross is not a geographically defined area – essentially it is the western part of the old county of Ross & Cromarty – but its characteristics are clear to anyone who has been there: it is a big, empty area full of craggy, singular hills enclosing narrow glens with deep inland lochs, backing a coast of long sea lochs, islands and low cliffs. It is also an excellent place for walking.

This particular guide covers the southern part of Wester Ross – from the southern end of Loch Maree in the north to Loch Carron in the south – and the area loosely described as 'Lochalsh' – the peninsulas to north and south of Loch Alsh.

There are only three ways into the area by road: down the coast from the north, via Loch Maree; from Dingwall to the east (both A832); and north-west from the Great Glen (A87). In addition, there is a railway line between Inverness and Kyle of Lochalsh. There are few minor roads, and anyone spending any time in the area will come to know the main routes well.

   The walks in this guide are in four distinct areas. Starting from the north, the bulk of the longer walks are in the hills around the head of Loch Torridon. This is classic Wester Ross scenery, with massive, rocky mountains towering over empty glens. The waymarked walks on the slopes of Beinn Eighe are worth visiting *(9)*, as they are the only walks in the guide which pass through the type of pine woodland which would once have covered the entire area (for walks at the north end of Loch Maree and beyond, see the companion volume *Walks Wester Ross: Northern Area*). South and west of that are a number of longer lineal walks. The three linked routes behind the stratified mass of Liathach are classics *(1,2,3)* – with the climb to Loch Coire Mhic Fhearchair being particularly dramatic – while the string of hill crossings between Glen Torridon and Glen Carron are all challenging. The most easterly – via Loch Coulin – is comparatively low-level and wooded, and follows a clear track *(8)*; the three paths joining at Bealach na Lice are harder walking through rockier terrain *(4,5,6)*. If you are looking for more gentle walking, there is a fine, short coastal circuit from the delightful village of Sheildaig *(10)*, plus two linked walks through the commercial conifers north of the mouth of Loch Carron *(16,17)*.

   The second distinct area is the Applecross peninsula, jutting westwards between Loch Torridon and Loch Carron. This is a big, empty area with a tiny population spread around the coast – mostly in the village by Applecross House. The roads in are narrow, steep and winding, so that it is a significant journey just to reach the start of the walks, but it is worth the effort. (The southern climb over Bealach na Bà is justly famous.) There is a network of low-level paths through the grazing land and woodland near the house *(12,14)*, plus a short, lineal walk to a splendid beach *(13)* and a longer hill crossing linking with the northern road in *(11)*. In addition, there is a moderate climb to a hill loch starting from the east end of the Bealach na Bà road *(15)*.

   The third area is the peninsula between Loch Carron and Loch Alsh. There are no towns with a population over a thousand in the area covered by this guide, but one of the largest settlements is Kyle of Lochalsh, on the end of this headland and at the east end of the bridge to Skye. This is the main service centre for the area. A lineal walk heads east from the village *(25)* and links with the waymarked walks through the birch woodland and commercial forestry around Balmacara Square *(24)*.

North of Kyle of Lochalsh, along a series of narrow minor roads, is the beautiful little village of Plockton, by its wooded bay. The village is a magnet for visitors, so arrive early if you want to find parking during the summer. There is a cluster of walks in the area: three short routes from the village itself *(19,20,21)*; two very short walks to picturesque bays nearby *(22)*; and a modest hill climb to a viewpoint in the woods to the south *(18)*. In addition, there is a short coast walk passing the little hamlet of Portneora, just to the south *(23)*.

Heading inland along Loch Alsh you reach the village of Dornie and the spectacular Eilean Donan Castle, sitting on its island – probably the best-known view in the area. There is a long, high-level moorland walk behind Dornie, providing fine views of the castle *(27)*, while further inland, beyond the head of Loch Duich, there is a lineal walk up the dramatic glen to the east of the line of hills known as the Five Sisters of Kintail *(26)*.

The final distinct area in the guide is the peninsula between Loch Alsh and Loch Duich to the north and Loch Hourn to the south. Just as with Applecross, it is a long drive in down a single-track road, but worth the trip. A major attraction of this area are its brochs – ancient, cylindrical dry-stone forts. The remains of one can be seen on the walk from the end of the road to the south of Loch Duich *(28)*, but the classic examples are in Gleann Beag, just south of Glenelg and well worth a visit. As for walks, there is a fine varied circuit leading to a remote settlement at Ardintoul and returning along the coast, with fine views over to the Isle of Skye *(10)*, a short, steep walk through conifers to the site of Gavin Maxwell's house at Sandaig (made famous by the book *Ring of Bright Water*) *(30)*, and a short coastal walk from the end of the road by Loch Hourn – a quiet and beautiful place *(31)*.

Edal memorial at Sandaig (Walk 30)

1 Allt a' Bhealaich /
2 Coire Mhic Nòbuil to Coire Mhic Fhearchair /
3 Loch Coire Mhic Fhearchair —————— A/A/A

Three connected routes through the spectacular hill scenery of Torridon. These routes can be walked individually or as one long walk. All paths are rough and occasionally faint. **1)** *Length:* **4 miles/6.5km** (there and back); *Height Climbed:* **1,213ft/370m**. **2)** *Length:* **8 miles/13km** (one way); *Height Climbed:* **1,213ft/370m** (from west), **1,107ft/310m** (from east). **3)** *Length:* **8 miles/13km** (there and back); *Height Climbed:* **1,670ft/510m**.

O.S. Sheet 19, 24 & 25

There are two car parks for these paths: one at Coire Dubh (6 miles west of Kinlochewe on the A896) and one at Coire Mhic Nòbuil (2 miles west of Torridon on the narrow road to the north of Upper Loch Torridon).

Walk 1) The Coire Mhic Nòbuil walk is the shortest of the three. Initially the path is clear: passing through a pine wood, while the river to the left of the path cuts through a narrow gorge overhung with rhododendrons, and with a fine waterfall at its upper end.

The path leaves the trees through a gate in a deer fence. Continue across moorland to a footbridge over the river, just after the confluence with Allt a' Bhealaich. Cross this.

Keep left at a junction marked by a cairn (go right here for Walk 2) and follow the path beside Allt a' Bhealaich, eventually crossing it by a wooden bridge and continuing. Keep right at the next junction (cairn) and continue into the gap between Beinn Alligin and Beinn Dearg. From here there are splendid views.

Return by the same route.

Walk 2) The path from Coire Mhic Nòbuil to Coire Dubh starts in the same way, but after crossing the Abhainn Coire Mhic Nòbuil go right at a junction (cairn) and follow a clear path up the valley between Liathach and Beinn Dearg. (For the Coire Dubh start, *see* Walk 3.) From this path there is a splendid view of Liathach's sharp, turreted ridge. The path is very rough in places, but clear. Keep straight on (ie, right) at the junction on the watershed behind Liathach. A little beyond the watershed the path crosses the Allt a' Choire Dhuibh Mhòir and skirts around the easterly buttress of the mountain, down to the road in Glen Torridon.

Walk 3) The path from Coire Dubh to Coire Mhic Fhearchair is the steepest and roughest of the three, but leads to the most dramatic and extensive views. Starting from the Coire Dubh car park, follow the clear, steep path signposted for Coire Mhich Nòbuil.

Just at the watershed, about 2$^{1}/_{2}$ miles/4km from the start, the path splits by a large cairn. Take the right-hand track, edging round the rocky lower slopes of Sàil Mhór to find a filmy waterfall over a wide shelf of rock between it and Ruadh-stac Mór.

Follow the track up the right-hand side of the shelf of rock. Behind it is little Loch Coire Mhic Fhearchair, dominated by the twin peaks to the east and west and the pleated Triple Buttress to the south. This is a place of awesome beauty.

Return by the same route.

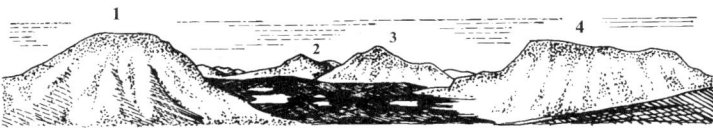

1 Beinn Dearg *(914m)* **2** Baosbheinn *(875m)* **3** Beinn an Eòin *(855m)* **4** Beinn a' Chearcaill *(725m)*

4 Torridon to Bealach na Lice / 5 Coulags to Bealach na Lice / 6 Achnashellach to Bealach na Lice ──────────────── A+/A+/A+

Three converging paths, meeting in a rocky hill pass in dramatic mountain scenery. Each can be walked there and back, or joined with one of the other routes to make a longer walk. All paths are clear, but very rough in places. **4)** *Length:* **5 miles/8km** (one way); *Height Climbed:* **1,410ft/430m**. **5)** *Length:* **5 miles/8km** (one way); *Height Climbed:* **1,312ft/400m**. **6)** *Length:* **6 miles/9.5km** (one way); *Height Climbed:* **1,800ft/550m**.

There is a possible rough, steep circuit around Maol Chean-dearg, which can be added to any of the routes (see map).

O.S. Sheet 24 & 25

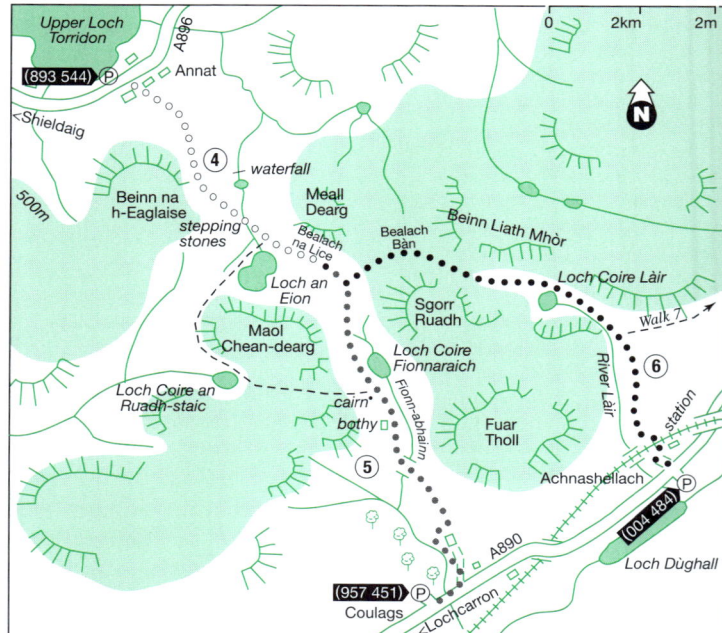

Walk 4) The route south from Loch Torridon starts at Annat, 6 miles east of Shieldaig on the A896. If arriving from that direction, the parking area is to the left of the road, just before the village sign.

Walk a few paces towards the houses and a sign points right for Coulags. There is a drive leading to a house, but you take the path to the left of that. A metal gate is visible ahead, level with the house, but before you reach it a sign points left for the hill path. This leads to a gate and then up and across the moorland slope.

The rough, clear path climbs then swings right, around the slope of Beinn na h-Eaglaise, and becomes less steep. Continue climbing, passing lochans and crossing a burn on large stepping stones.

There is a further climb with a slope to the left to reach Loch an Eion, in the corrie between Meall Dearg and Maol Chean-dearg. On the near side of the loch the path splits. To reach Bealach na Lice, keep to the left of the lochan and follow the path up to the col beyond.

Walk 5) Coulags is 5 miles east of Lochcarron on the A890. Park in the car park to the west of the burn then cross the burn and turn left, off the road, at a sign for the path.

The walking route bypasses Coulags Lodge then continues up the east side of the river. $1^{1}/_{2}$ miles/2.5km from Coulags the path crosses the river on a bridge and then continues up the west bank, passing the Coire Fionnaraich bothy. Beyond this the path – now rougher and damper – continues up the glen. Watch for a junction marked by a cairn – the start of the path around Maol Chean-dearg (*see* map). For the main route, continue up the glen to little Loch Coire Fionnaraich before skirting around the headwaters of the glen and cutting west into Bealach na Lice.

Walk 6) The toughest of the three paths is the route from Achnashellach Station – 8 miles east of Lochcarron on the A890. Park in the lay-by opposite the start of the entrance track.

Follow the track up to the station and cross the railway (carefully). Beyond, the track climbs to a four-way junction. Go back-left (Coire Làir). You quickly pass through the line of a deer fence and walk on along a track through conifers. After 600 paces a green arrow points left, off the track. Follow this downhill then go right, with a fence to your right and the River Làir down to the left.

The trees end and the fence heads off to the right. The clear path now climbs steeply until it levels out in the upper corrie. Paths head first left then right (*see* walk 7) at cairned junctions, but just keep straight on up the glen to reach Loch Coire Làir.

Beyond the loch the glen narrows between Beinn Liath Mhòr and Sgorr Ruadh, and the path becomes rocky and steep, finally reaching a narrow and most dramatic pass at the point where the two hills meet. The path then makes a rocky and precipitous descent into the neighbouring glen before cutting left (south-west), across Bealach Bàn, and then right (west), into Bealach na Lice.

7 **Achnashellach Loop** _____ A

This walk is connected to Walks 6 and 8, but allows you to make a loop – through conifer woodland and over open moorland – rather than a hill-crossing. Clear tracks and rough paths. Length: **8 miles/13km***; Total Height Climbed:* **1,700ft/520m**.

O.S. Sheet 25

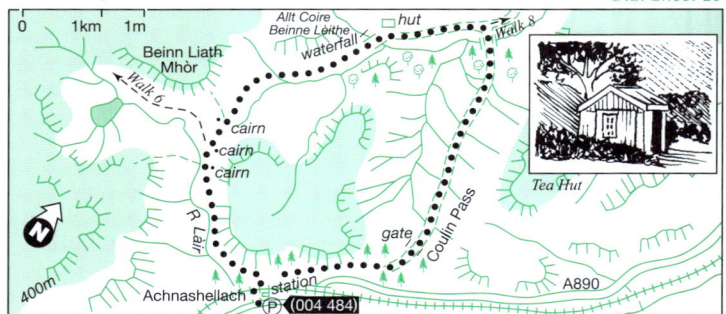

Park at Achnashellach and start this walk as instructed for Walk 6. Follow the directions until you have left the conifer woodland and made the steep climb above the River Làir to reach the upper glen.

Near the top of the steep section you reach a junction marked by a cairn, with a path heading off to your left. Ignore this and continue to reach a junction by a second cairn, visible ahead. This time, go right.

You are now walking northeast, with the steep slope of Beinn Liath Mhòr to your left. After a short distance there is another junction by a cairn, with a path heading left to climb the face of the hill. Ignore that and keep to the right.

A clear path continues across the moorland before beginning to descend with a burn down to your right and mixed birch and pine woodland on the far side of the glen. This leads to a footbridge over Allt Coire Beinne Lèithe, just below a waterfall, with the Tea Hut (a bothy) just beyond.

A clear track now runs down the glen for a mile/1.6km to reach a junction with a track (*see* Walk 8) crossing the river on a bridge to your right. Cross the bridge and follow the track out of the woodland and on up the glen to Coulin Pass at its head.

Go through a gate in a deer fence to enter a large conifer plantation. Follow the track as it leads downhill then swings to the right (ignore a signposted path heading off to the left) and continues down and across the slope towards Achnashellach.

When you reach the junction just above the station, retrace your steps to the start.

8 Achnashellach to Loch Clair _____ A

A lineal hill-crossing, starting through commercial woodland, crossing open moorland, then finishing through pleasant mixed woodland by inland lochs. Clear tracks and rough footpaths. Length: **9 miles/14.5km** (one way); *Height Climbed:* **820ft/250m**.

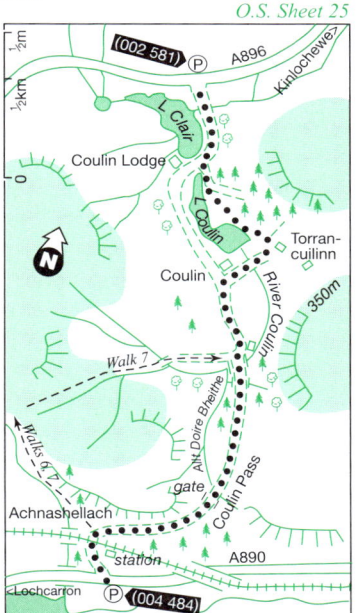

The two terminuses of this path are at Achnashellach Station (on the A890, 8 miles east of Lochcarron) and Loch Clair (3 miles south of Kinlochewe on the A896). There are small car parks by the road at each end.

Starting from Achnashellach, cross the road from the car park and follow the track uphill to the station. Cross the railway (with care) and continue a short way uphill to reach a four-way junction. For this walk, take the forestry road going up and across the slope (Torridon by Coulin Pass).

The track climbs through conifers for a little over a mile/1.6km, then edges left and completes the last climb to a gate in a deer fence on the edge of the trees.

Beyond this there is a 2 mile/3.2km descent on a rough track down the glen of Allt Doire Bheithe; through moorland at first, then through a pleasant woodland of birch and pine. This leads to the bridge over the River Coulin. On the far side there is a T-junction. Go right.

The clear track runs a little over a mile/1.6km to a junction by the house at Coulin. Go right (footpath), heading towards the buildings at Torrancuilinn on the far side of the glen.

Cross a bridge over the river and follow the track beyond, passing to the left of the buildings and heading for the edge of a conifer plantation. Before you reach the trees the track crosses a small burn and a signposted path then heads off to the left.

Turn on to this rough path and follow it along Loch Coulin to join a clear track near its far end. Continue along this track; down the side of Loch Clair, across a bridge and up to the public road.

9 Beinn Eighe Trails _____ A/C

Two waymarked walks: one a short loop through mature Scots pine woodland; the longer climbing above the trees to give spectacular views of the surrounding mountains. Paths rough and steep in places.
Length: **1-4 miles/1.6-6.5km**; *Height Climbed:* **330-1,800ft/100-550m**.

O.S. Sheet 19

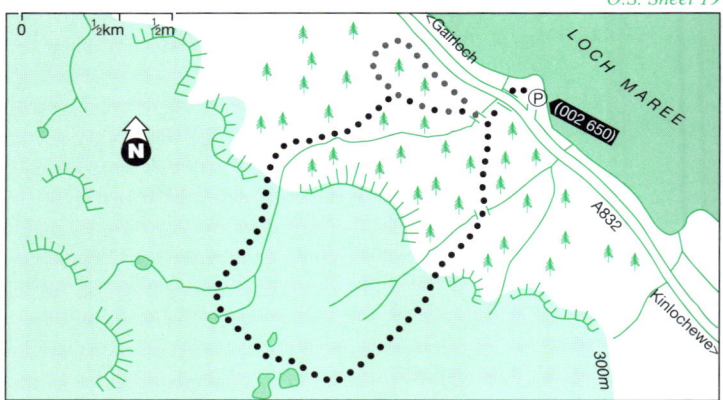

Beinn Eighe is south-west of the southern end of Loch Maree. The car park for the nature trails is by the side of the loch, 2½ miles north of Kinlochewe on the A832.

Beinn Eighe is a National Nature Reserve, of interest due to both the mature Scots pine woodland of its lower slopes and its bare summits. This type of ground cover – which once would have covered much of this area – is now rare. Indeed, this is the only walk in this guide which passes through a significant area of native pine woodland. Information on the wildlife and geology of the area is available from the visitor centre (2 miles along the A832 towards Kinlochewe).

The two trails start by passing under the road by the side of the burn at the far end of the car park. Immediately beyond the road the trails split: for the short, woodland trail go right (marked by a tree symbol), across a footbridge; for the longer, mountain trail go straight on (mountain).

Both routes involve climbing and rough paths, but while the short route stays entirely within the forest, the longer route climbs above the trees to a high plateau dotted with lochans, providing splendid views. This route is steep in places, and care must be taken to follow the cairns and stone plaques which mark the route.

10 **Shieldaig** ─────────────────── B

A lineal walk round a rocky headland, following clear tracks and rough paths. Some scrambling in places. Fine views of Loch Torridon and the surrounding peaks. Length: **3 miles/5km**; *Height Climbed: undulating.*

O.S. Sheet 24

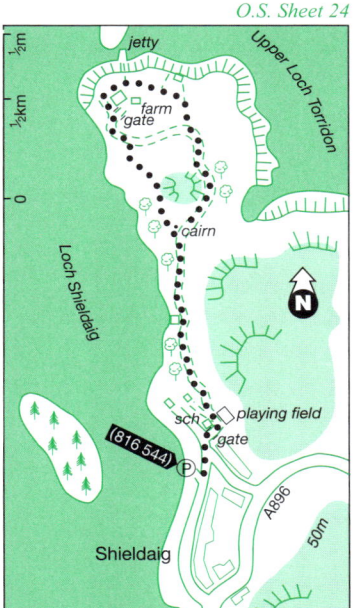

Shieldaig is a picturesque little village four miles west of the head of Loch Torridon, at the point where the A896 turns south, away from the loch. There is a car park behind the shore, near the north end of the village.

Walk north from the car park (ie, with the sea to your left) and you quickly reach a hairpin bend. There is a four-way junction here. Leave the main road and take the tarred road to the right of the primary school.

You quickly reach a junction by a playing field. Go left (Rubha Lodge). Just beyond the end of the playing field there is a third junction. Go right this time and follow a clear track out along the headland. Continue on the track to reach a junction marked by a large cairn. Go left here, leaving the main track, and following a rough path.

A series of painted white arrows lead up the rocks in front of you. From the top of the slope the path is clear but rough in places and runs on with woodland to your left before dropping to reach a further junction with the clear track.

Go left, and follow the track (detours to the left to viewpoints are marked by white dots along the next section). As you approach a farm the path splits. Go left, then right and follow the fence around the buildings. There are no markers here, but aim to climb towards a wind turbine on the low hill above the farm. A chain helps you up the steepest part.

Once on the top, the path crosses a low hill. Ignore paths off to the left and descend to join a grassy path climbing from a house down to your left. Turn right along this and follow it to a junction with the clear track.

Turn left and follow the track back to the start.

11 Applecross to Kenmore ——————————— A+

A long lineal walk across moorland, following a clear track and rough paths. The route is generally clear, but a map will be needed. Length: **9 miles/14.5km** (one way); *Height Climbed:* **820ft/250m**.

O.S. Sheet 24

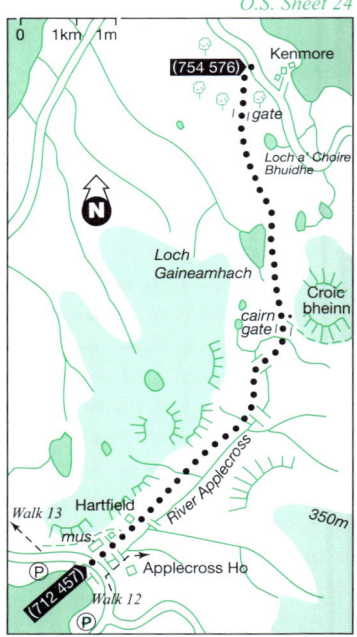

Follow the instructions for Walk 12 to reach Applecross then park in the village (*see* map).

Walk to the bridge crossing the River Applecross and turn on to the metalled road on the north side of the river, signposted as the path to Kenmore. After a short distance there is a bridge to the right carrying a road to Applecross House. Ignore this and continue by the river. When the main track turns left, into the hostel and bunkhouse at Hartfield, keep straight on along a clear track.

After a short distance a bridge crosses the river to your right. Ignore this and continue on the track up the glen.

3 miles/5km from the road the track crosses a burn and becomes rougher, then crosses a bridge to your right. Ignore this and keep straight on along a rough path up the left-hand side of a tributary; climbing and swinging to the north (left).

The path climbs to a flatter area then continues for a short way before crossing the tributary on a footbridge. After a further ¹/₂ mile/0.8km it recrosses the burn and goes through a gate in a deer fence. Just beyond this there is a split in the path, marked by a cairn. Keep left, with the steep slope of Croic bheinn to your right.

The path now runs straight, passing Loch Gaineamhach, before descending across the slope above Loch a' Choire Bhuidhe, providing a spectacular view across Loch Torridon to the north. When you reach a fence running down the slope, follow it downhill for a short distance then go left, through a metal gate, and continue through mixed woodland to reach the road near the village of Kenmore.

12 Applecross House Walks —————————————————— C

A short walk through the woodland surrounding Applecross House, making use of some of the waymarked paths in the area. Paths are good, though some care is needed with navigation. Length: **3 miles/5km**; *Height Climbed:* **165ft/50m**. *Possible link with Walk 14.*

O.S. Sheet 24

Applecross House, on the west side of the Applecross peninsula, is accessible from either Shieldaig or Kishorn by the dramatic road which leads round the big headland. It is a long drive in, and you should always leave plenty of time for the journey.

Look for the signs for the Walled Garden and follow the driveway up to the car park by the walled garden. (It is also possible to park in the village.) Walk on beyond the car park, with the garden off to your left. After 90 paces you reach a four-way junction, with an old ice house directly ahead. Go right.

The path passes through two gates before joining the driveway, to which it has been running roughly parallel. Follow the drive to the road. Just before you join the road a path heads off to the left – a possible ½ mile/0.8km link with Walk 14 – but for this walk turn right, along the road.

On the near side of the bridge over the River Applecross turn right, through a gate, and follow a rough path to the right of the river. Cross an access road to the main house, with a bridge to your left, and continue by the river (Roes' Walk).

The path edges right and starts climbing by a tributary. After passing through three gates the path climbs to a signposted junction by a set of stone

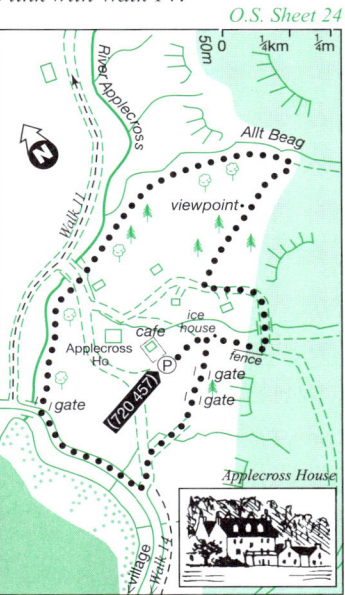

steps. Go back-right, up a slope, and follow the path past a viewpoint and on to a junction with a clear track.

Go left here (Keppoch). Keep straight on past the entrance to a house to your right. Just ahead, the track swings right, crosses a bridge, then goes left. At that point head right (Walled Garden), on a path with a fence to your left. This leads back to the junction by the Ice House.

13 Applecross to Sand ────────── B

A hill track with terrific sea views leading to a fine sandy beach. Length:
3¼ miles/5.25km (one way); *Height Climbed:* **500ft/150m**.

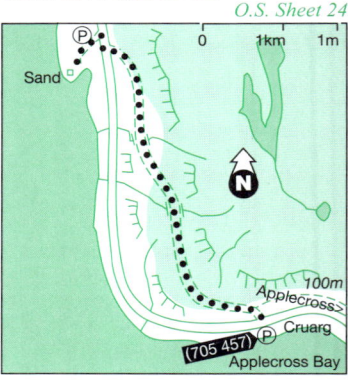

This route starts at a car park on the northern side of Applecross Bay. A clear path starts on the far side of the road. Follow this up to a signposted junction. Go left (Sand).

Follow the clear path as it climbs steadily above the bay with fine views to Rona and Raasay. The route is never in doubt – the track levels out to cross undulating moorland before dropping to join the public road above Sand. Turn right on the road for a short distance to reach the car park and entrance road to the beach. Return by the same route.

14 Milton Circuit ────────── C

A short circuit from Applecross on tracks, rough paths and public roads. Length: **2 miles/3km**; *Height Climbed:* **160ft/50m**.

Park at the car park in the village in Applecross, walk back out of the car park and go left for a short distance then head right, uphill, on the Lochcarron road (careful of traffic).

After 100 paces go right, off the road, on a clear path. This short path climbs to a junction. Go right, with farm buildings to your right, to reach a gate in a deer fence. Go through this and continue on the clear track, eventually passing through dense conifer woods.

You emerge from the trees at a cottage (Torgarve) and the track ends. Go right, round the cottage, to pick up a faint path heading half right towards the sea. This drops to join a clear track to the left of a cottage by a small loch. Go right and follow the track to the public road. Go right and follow this (carefully) back to the start.

15 Loch Gaineamhach ─────────────────── B

A rough, lineal path, climbing through open moorland to a hill loch flanked by dramatic mountains. Length: **6 miles/10km** (there and back)*; Height Climbed:* **890ft/270m**. *The path is clear, but in wet weather some of the burns will need to be forded. Fine views.*

O.S. Sheets 24

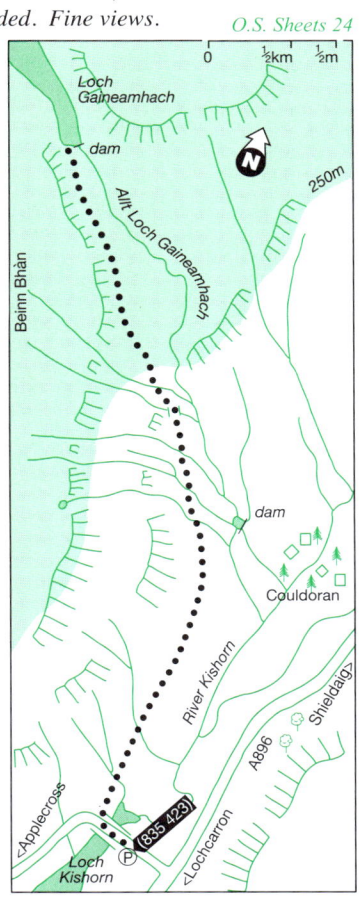

To reach the start of this route, drive 5 miles west from Lochcarron on the A896 to reach the junction with the minor road to Applecross (the Bealach na Bà road). Turn left on to this. The road runs straight for a short distance to cross the River Kishorn. Just before the bridge there is room to park to the left of the road.

Walk across the bridge. Immediately beyond it, a rough, clear path starts to the right of the road.

The route is never in doubt. The path starts by running across the slope, climbing slowly, with the River Kishorn down to the right. After passing the trees and buildings at Couldoran, however, down to your right, it swings left and begins a steeper climb above the Allt Loch Gaineamhach. The path crosses a number of small tributaries. The largest is crossed by a bridge; the others will need to be jumped or forded.

As you climb, views begin to open up of the spectacular string of corries and buttresses of Beinn Bhàn, up to your left. To the right, the slope is a mix of moorland and bare rock.

After a final steep ascent, the loch comes in to view, with a low dam at its near end. The path stops here. More experienced and adventurous walkers may choose to explore the slopes of Beinn Bhàn, but for this walk, return by the same route.

Walks Wester Ross: Southern Area

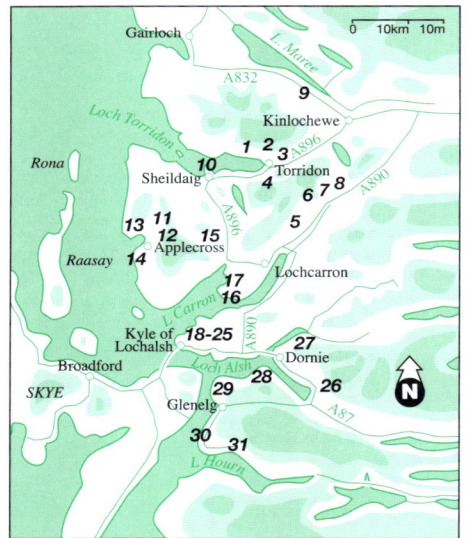

Grades

A+ ... Full walking equipment – including map and compass – and previous hill walking experience essential

A ...... Full walking equipment required

B ...... Strong walking footwear and waterproof clothing required

C ...... Comfortable walking footwear recommended

NB: Assume each walk increases at least one grade in winter conditions. Hill routes can become treacherous.

— www.pocketwalks.com —

Published by: *Hallewell Publications, Scotland*
Printed by: *Barr Printers Ltd, Glenrothes*

While every care has been taken in the preparation of this guide, the publishers cannot accept responsibility for any loss, damage or injury resulting from its use.

Walks Wester Ross: Southern Area

walk	grade
1 Allt a' Bhealaich	A
2 Coire Mhic Nòbuil to Coire Mhic Fhearchair	A
3 Loch Coire Mhic Fhearchair	A
4 Torridon to Bealach na Lice	A+
5 Coulags to Bealach na Lice	A+
6 Achnashellach to Bealach na Lice	A+
7 Achnashellach Loop	A
8 Achnashellach to Loch Clair	A
9 Beinn Eighe Trails	A/C
10 Shieldaig	B
11 Applecross to Kenmore	A+
12 Applecross House Walks	C
13 Applecross to Sand	B
14 Milton Circuit	C
15 Loch Gaineamhach	B
16 Leacanasigh	B
17 Leacanasigh to Achintraid	B
18 Carn a' Bhealaich Mhòir	B
19 The Brae	C
20 Duncraig Castle	C
21 Carn na Frith-Aird	C
22 Plockton Beaches	C
23 Portneora	B
24 Two Walks from Balmacara Square	B/A
25 Kyle of Lochalsh to Balmacara	B
26 Glenlicht	A
27 Loch Long & Loch Duich	A+
28 Caisteal Grugaig	B
29 Ardintoul	A
30 Sandaig	B
31 Corran	B

16 Leacanasigh / 17 Leacanasigh to Achintraid _ B/B

16) *A short circuit, starting through conifer forest then returning by the coast. Paths rough and steep in places. Length:* **4½ miles/7km**; *Height Climbed:* **330ft/100m**. **17)** *A lineal hill crossing, through conifers and over open moorland. Fine views. Length:* **6 miles/10km** *(there and back); Total Height Climbed:* **660ft/200m**.

O.S. Sheet 24

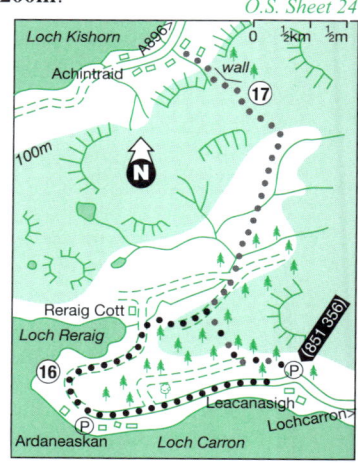

These two walks can be walked individually or combined. Walk 17 can be walked in either direction, but parking is difficult at the north end.

Walks 16 & 17) To reach Leacanasigh take the North Strone road from Lochcarron. After 3½ miles the road enters a wood. The walk starts up the slope opposite a small group of houses just beyond a cattle grid, and there is a small car park at the start of the path. (If this is full, park at Ardaneaskan, also on Walk 16).

Cut up across a wooded slope. The path is clear and soon joins a forestry track. After 130 paces a rough footpath, marked by a sign/cairn, cuts right from the track, climbing through the forest. Follow this path over a low watershed and down into the valley of the Reraig Burn, where the path reaches a junction with a forest road. Here you have a choice.

Walk 16) To return to the start, turn left (Reraig). When the track ends, continue on a path, descending trough trees to run to the left of a fence. The path ends at a gate into the field to your right. Go through the gate and follow the line of the fence down to the shore. Go left on a clear track along the edge of the tidal Loch Reraig, then round the headland to Ardaneaskan. Follow the public road back to the start.

Walk 17) Go right for 500 paces to reach a junction. Keep straight on. After a short distance a signposted path (Achintraid) heads off to the left.

The path is perfectly clear; climbing through mixed woodland at first, then over the open moor. From the top of the hill there are fine views of the mountains of Applecross to the north. Beyond the highest point the path descends, edges right to join a wall, then runs straight down the slope, by a burn, to Achintraid.

18 Carn a' Bhealaich Mhòir _____B

A circuit, on clear tracks and public roads, through conifer woodland and passing two lochs, with a spur path climbing steeply to a fine viewpoint. Length: **7 miles/11km**; *Height Climbed:* **820ft/250m**.

O.S. Sheet 24

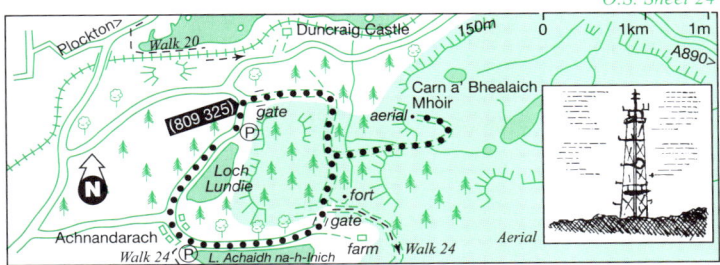

If you look south-east from Plockton you will see a heather-topped hill with a prominent aerial rising from the conifer woods. This is Carn a' Bhealaich Mhòir. If driving to Plockton by the northern route (ie, following the minor roads from the A890 by Strome Ferry), watch for the entrance to Duncraig Castle to the right then keep left at the next junction.

After a short distance you pass a track entrance to the left of the road. This is the start of the walk, but continue for a further 300m and park in a space to the left of the road.

Walk back down the road and start walking up the track (path sign). When a signposted path cuts left (Duncraig), ignore this and continue on the main track, which soon bends right and continues to a three-way junction.

To continue the climb, go left (viewpoint). The track descends then climbs steeply to the top of the hill. From the summit cairn, there are wonderful views over Plockton to Raasay and the hills of Skye, Wester Ross and Kintail.

Return to the junction and turn left (ie, keep straight on if you are not making the climb). Follow the clear track down towards Loch Achaidh na h-Inich. As you descend, there is an interpretive panel to the left of the track (a brief diversion at this point climbs to the site of an iron-age fort).

As you approach the loch you reach a four-way junction (a link with Walk 24). For this walk, go straight across then down, through a gate, to reach the end of the narrow public road by the entrance to a farm.

Veer right and follow the road by the lochside. At the end of the loch the road passes a small parking area then continues through the scattered settlement of Achnandarach.

Keep right at the junction beyond to return to the start.

19 The Brae / 20 Duncraig Castle / 21 Carn na Frith-Aird ———————— C/C/C

Three walks starting from the village of Plockton. **19)** *A short, easy circuit using a track above the village. Length:* **1 mile/1.6km**; *Height Climbed:* **130ft/40m**. **20)** *A low, lineal path, through woodland by the shore, providing fine views. Length:* **4 miles/6.5km** (there and back); *Height Climbed: undulating.* **21)** *A short lineal climb, on roads and a rough path, to a fine viewpoint. Length:* **1 mile/1.6km** (there and back); *Height Climbed:* **100ft/30m**.

O.S. Sheet 24

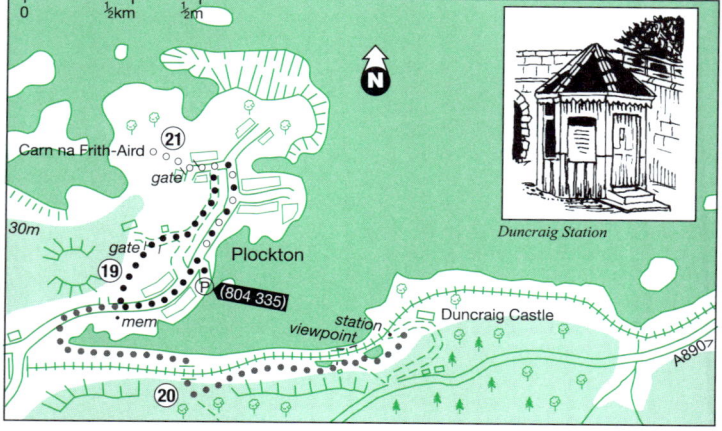

Duncraig Station

The pretty village of Plockton sits on the southern edge of the entrance to Loch Carron, with fine views of the surrounding sea, forests and mountains. It can be reached via a bewildering (but signposted) series of minor roads from either Kyle of Lochalsh or off the A890, just south of Strome Ferry. The public road enters the village from the south. Look for a sign for the car park to the right and park behind the shore.

Walks 19 & 20) Start walking back along Innes Street – the road into the village. The road leaves the houses and climbs. At the top of the first climb there is a sign pointing right for The Brae.

Walk 19) Turn right here and start climbing on a rough path. A fine view opens up and you can see both Duncraig Castle (Walk 20) and Carn a' Bhealaich Mhòir (Walk 18). Follow the path over a low hill, through heather, rock and scattered pine trees, before joining an S-shaped driveway at a pedestrian gate.

Turn right along the driveway, which runs straight to reach the top of the slope above Plockton. A track heads off back-right at this point; ignore this and continue along the clearer track, which edges left to run along the top of the slope.

Follow this track – enjoying the fine views of the village and the bay below – until it ends at the public road (Frithard Rd). Turn right to return to the start through the village, or left to join Walk 21.

Walk 20) Continue up the road. Almost immediately you pass the entrance to the war memorial on the left, then the entrance to a 19th-century open-air church to the right. Continue, with a tidal inlet down to your left.

The inlet ends and houses appear ahead, to the right of the road. Look for a sign to the left ('Duncraig Castle') and follow a clear path across the head of the inlet and down the far side through woodland. There are fine views.

The path climbs to run parallel to a railway line then passes beneath it. Beyond this the path climbs. After 130 paces you reach a signposted junction. Turn left (Duncraig), off the main track; passing through a gate and following a rough path through trees and rhododendrons.

You reach a small pond, where water has seeped through beneath the railway, with a ruin at the far end. A brief diversion to the left at this point, under the railway, leads to a fine viewpoint.

Return to the original path and continue to a clear junction. Turn left here, towards a level-crossing over the railway. Just before the crossing turn right, on to a path through rhododendrons. This leads to a larger lagoon, fed through a bridge carrying the railway.

At the far end of the inlet the path becomes a track and climbs to join a metalled road. A brief diversion to the right leads to a view of the castle (private), built in 1866 for the businessman Sir Alexander Matheson. Double back and follow the metalled road (keep left at a fork) down to the station, which was created purely for the use of the castle.

Return by the same route.

Walk 21) This route can be walked as an extension to Walk 19. If you are walking it on its own, leave the car park and walk on along the sea front, on Harbour St. When this road ends, turn left on Frithard Rd.

The road runs straight for a short way then begins to swing round to the left. Just before it does so there is a sign to the right, pointing to the Carn na Frith-Aird viewpoint.

Go through a pedestrian gate and follow a rough, clear path through heather, birch, pine and rhododendrons to the low hill top, from where there is a fine view to Skye and Applecross, and a view indicator to describe it.

Return by the same route.

22 Plockton Beaches ——————————————————————C

Two short walks starting near Plockton Aerodrome and leading, on clear paths, to quiet beaches. Length: ¾ mile/1km *and* 1½ miles/2.5km (there and back); Height Climbed: *negligible.*

O.S. Sheet 24

To reach the start of these two walks, drive (or walk) ½ mile west from Plockton on the public road. Pass the High School and look for a road heading right, for the station. Turn onto this but don't go into the station – keep straight on past the entrance.

The road dog-legs to the right and runs straight for a short distance before a road cuts off to the left, signposted for 'Dubh Aird Beach Access'. This road joins the fence around the runway and edges left. At the end of the aerodrome runway it turns hard right, then hard right again. At this point there is a parking space to the left of the metalled road.

Port Lunga is a small, sheltered beach of coral sand. To reach it, walk back to the start of the parking area where there is a sign for the footpath to the shore.

Start along a very clear track, which ends by a caravan. Go through a gate here and continue along a clear, maintained path (watch out for cattle in this section) down to the grassy area behind the little beach.

Return by the same route.

The walk to **Camas Dubh Aird** is slightly longer, but the bay is a larger area of mud, rock and sand. To reach it, walk on beyond the parking area, with a bank of gorse between you and the runway to your right. There is a line of houses to the left of the metalled road. Immediately beyond the second house a clear track heads off to the left, signposted as a footpath to the shore.

The track ends at a field entrance. Continue on a path between fences to reach the shore. This is a rocky shore behind a muddy bay, which dries at low tide (watch out for the tide if you visit the little islands). If you want some sand, walk around to the right until a rough path leads across a neck of land to a small, north-facing beach.

Return by the same route.

23 Portneora

A short loop through farmland and along the rocky shore. The path is rough in places, but there are waymarks. Be wary of grazing cattle. Fine coastal views. Length: **2 miles/3km**; *Height Climbed:* undulating.

O.S. Sheet 24

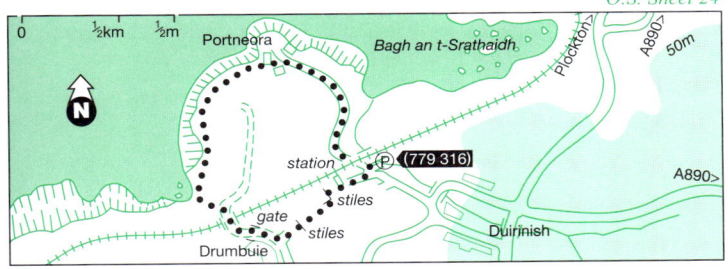

Portneora (sometimes 'Port an Eorna' on signs) is a small settlement behind a rocky bay on the coast west of Plockton. To reach the start of this walk, drive two miles west from Plockton following the signs for Duirinish. Turn right, to pass through the village, then follow the signs for Portneora.

After a short distance you reach the level crossing by Duirinish Station. When the road jinks left to cross the railway line keep straight on, along a rough track, and park immediately – making sure you don't block the track.

Walk back along the road (ie, don't cross the railway; that is your return route). You quickly reach a junction, with the public road heading left and a private road going straight on. Keep straight on, passing to the left of a terrace of cottages.

The track becomes a grassy path and continues along a low ridge.

After a short distance you cross a stile and head down to the left, to the corner of a field. Cross a stile over the fence ahead and turn right. At the end of the field, cross a stile, a bridge over a drainage ditch and a second stile (Coastal Walk), then cross a marshy area and climb a slope to join the public road amidst the houses of Drumbuie.

Turn right. Almost immediately you reach a gate with a large green shed beyond it. Go through the gate and follow the track past the shed and down to a bridge over the railway.

At the far end of the bridge turn left off the track (Port an eorna) and walk down the left-hand edges of two fields to reach a shingle beach.

Walk along the back of the beach, cross a rocky headland (waymarked) then continue along the shore until the rough path joins the public road at Portneora. Turn right to return to the start of the walk.

24 Two Walks from Balmacara Square —————— B/A

Two circuits from the small village of Balmacara Square. **A)** *A loop through woodland and across the open hill, giving fine views over Loch Alsh to Skye. Tracks and paths of varying quality, steep in places.* Length: **2½-4 miles/4-6.5km**; Height Climbed: **660ft/200m.** **B)** *A walk over a low hill through fine birchwoods, leading to a scenic loch and returning by forest roads. Good paths and clear tracks.* Length: **8 miles/13km**; Height Climbed: **1,300ft/400m.**

O.S. Sheet 24 & 33

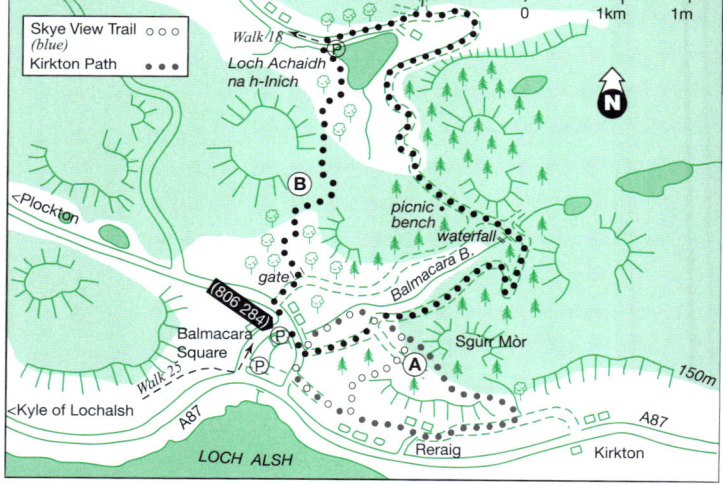

Balmacara Square is a small village to the east of Kyle of Lochalsh. There are two car parks as well as an NTS exhibition centre and café. A network of paths has been laid out through the woods around the village, linking with paths to Plockton and Kyle of Lochalsh (*see map and Walks 18 and 25*). The walks can be started from either car park. The routes described here start from the car park by the exhibition centre and give a sample of what is possible. A study of a map will show other options.

To reach the start, drive two miles east from Kyle of Lochalsh and turn off the main road at the sign for Balmacara Square. Park in the car park for the NTS exhibition centre.

A) For the shorter circuit, walk out of the far end of the car park and turn right along the public road (Forest

Walks). Immediately beyond a bridge over Balmacara Burn, there is a sign to the left for the forest walks, and a post with a blue band. Go through a pedestrian gate and follow a path back to the burn.

The path continues beside the burn initially then edges right and climbs to join a forest track. Turn left up the track. After a short distance, there is a post to the right of the track (Skye View Trail) and a rough path climbs steeply then contours along the slope to reach a waymarked split.

To shorten the walk go right and follow the blue 'Skye View Trail' (the path drops to cross a forest road, then continues over an open area), but for the longer route take the left-hand path (Kirkton) which runs across the slope with fine views.

Watch for a point where the path jinks to the right to join the line of an old wall, covered by moss. When the wall to your right ends, the path cuts right and zig-zags steeply downhill (take care), through fine oakwood then conifers, to join a path running along the foot of the wood.

A turn to the left leads to Kirkton, but for this walk go right. As you approach the houses at Reraig, the first house blocks the path. Go left, through a gate, to bypass it and rejoin the line of the path – now a metalled road – just beyond.

At the junction with the road coming up from the A87, keep straight on. Pass one house to your right then turn left off the metalled road onto a grassy path through bracken, marked by a post (footpath).

Follow this path across the slope, ignoring a signposted path heading left for Reraig at one point. $1/2$ mile/0.8km from Reraig you reach a junction in gorse bushes with a path coming in from behind-right. This is the blue route. Keep straight on and follow the clear path on between fields, ignoring gates to right and left, to reach the public road. Turn right along the road to return to the start.

B) Walk out of the car park and follow the public road north, uphill. Beyond the houses, the road swings left. Look for a wooden signpost to the right of the road at this point, marking the footpath to Achnahinich. Go right, through a gate and follow the clear track beyond.

Just after crossing a stream, go left through a kissing gate (Achnahinich) and follow the clear path which climbs through birchwoods then briefly out on to the open hill before descending through trees to the side of Loch Achaidh na h-Inich.

Follow the path by the loch to reach the public road by a small parking area. Go right and follow the road along the lochside. The road ends at a fork by a farm entrance. Go left, passing through a gate and following a clear track to a four-way junction. Go right (Balmacara) on a clear forest road.

As you climb, you pass a picnic bench (fine views). Keep straight on at a junction beyond (ie, ignore the 'Waterfall Route' to the right) and follow the clear forest road back down to the public road.

Turn right to return to the start.

25 Kyle of Lochalsh to Balmacara ──────── B

A lineal path, through mixed woodland and over open moorland, giving fine views over Loch Alsh to the surrounding mountains. The path is clear, but rough and damp in places. Length: **3 miles/5km** *(one way); Height Climbed:* **330ft/100m** *(undulating).*

O.S. Sheet 33

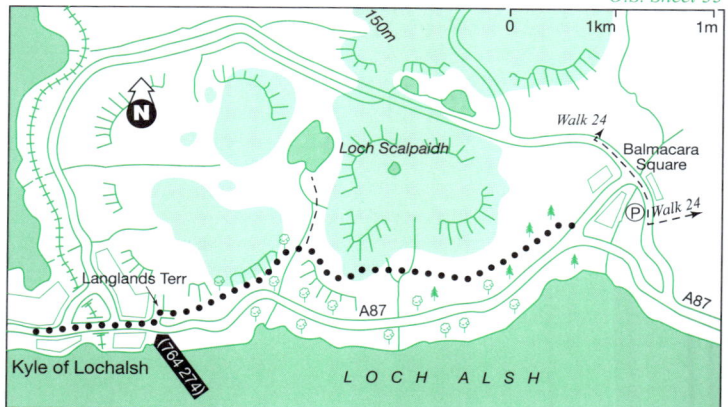

This rough path runs along the slope above the A87, linking Kyle of Lochalsh with the little village of Balmacara Square (where there is a possible link with Walk 24). If you can't get someone to pick you up at the far end, return by the same route.

From the centre of Kyle of Lochalsh, walk east on the A87. Cross the railway, pass the petrol station, then turn left up Langlands Terrace. Turn immediately right, onto a dead-end road. When the road ends continue over a grassy area to reach a sign at the start of the path.

The path climbs through bracken at first, then follows the line of an old pipe through heather moorland before entering a fine wood of birch and oak, with good views of the loch below.

The path heads inland, up a valley. At the point where the path crosses the burn there is a signposted junction. A detour to the left at this point will lead (via a wet path) to a good picnic spot by little Loch Scalpaidh. Otherwise, keep straight on (Balmacara); crossing rougher moorland, with rocky outcrops, before descending into conifer woodland.

The path comes down to run parallel to the road, crosses a wooden footbridge then continues to join the public road. Turn left here for half a mile to reach Balmacara Square; otherwise, return by the same route.

26 Glenlicht _____ A

A lineal, there-and-back walk up a dramatic glen, leading to a waterfall. A clear track for most of the way, with a section of rough footpath at the end. Length: **11 miles/17.5km** (there and back); Height Climbed: **660ft/200m**.

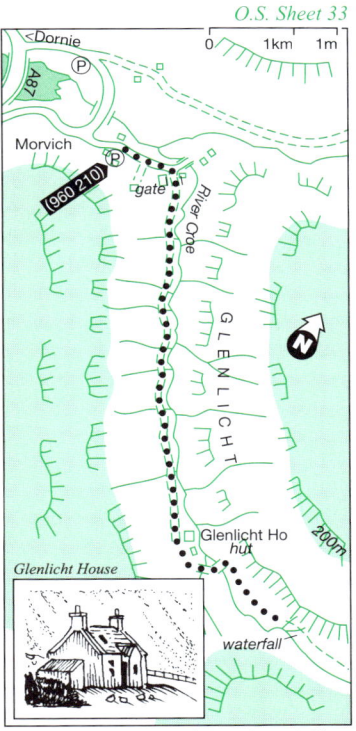

O.S. Sheet 33

To reach the start of this walk, drive 5 miles east from Dornie on the A87, through Inverinate, and turn left onto a minor road signed for Morvich. After about a mile the road crosses the River Croe. Turn left just beyond at the sign for the Kintail Countryside Centre. After a short distance there is a small car park by the buildings to the right of the road.

Walk on up the metalled road. At the first split keep left, by the river. At the next split, shortly beyond, go right (Glen Affric). The sign points to a gate to the left of a large shed. Go through the pedestrian gate beside this and start walking up the clear track beyond.

There is no doubt about the route: the track runs straight up the glen with Beinn Fhada ahead and to your left and the Five Sisters of Kintail to your right. After 4 miles/6.5km you reach the climbers' hut at Glenlicht (the main hut is kept locked, but there is a shelter for walkers at the end of the building).

If you want to avoid the steep climb, just turn back from here. If you wish to see the waterfall, follow a rough path past a ruin and down to a footbridge over a burn. Cross this and continue to reach a second footbridge, over a deep gorge.

Beyond this the path climbs steeply up the side of the glen. A little over a mile/1.6km from the second bridge the glen narrows and there is a dramatic waterfall in a rocky bowl ahead.

Return by the same route.

27 Loch Long & Loch Duich ———————— A+

This is a long, rough, steep route giving fine views. Paths are faint in places, so some navigation will be required. The return is along a quiet public road. **Length: 12 miles/19km**; **Height Climbed: 1,700ft/520m**.

O.S. Sheet 33

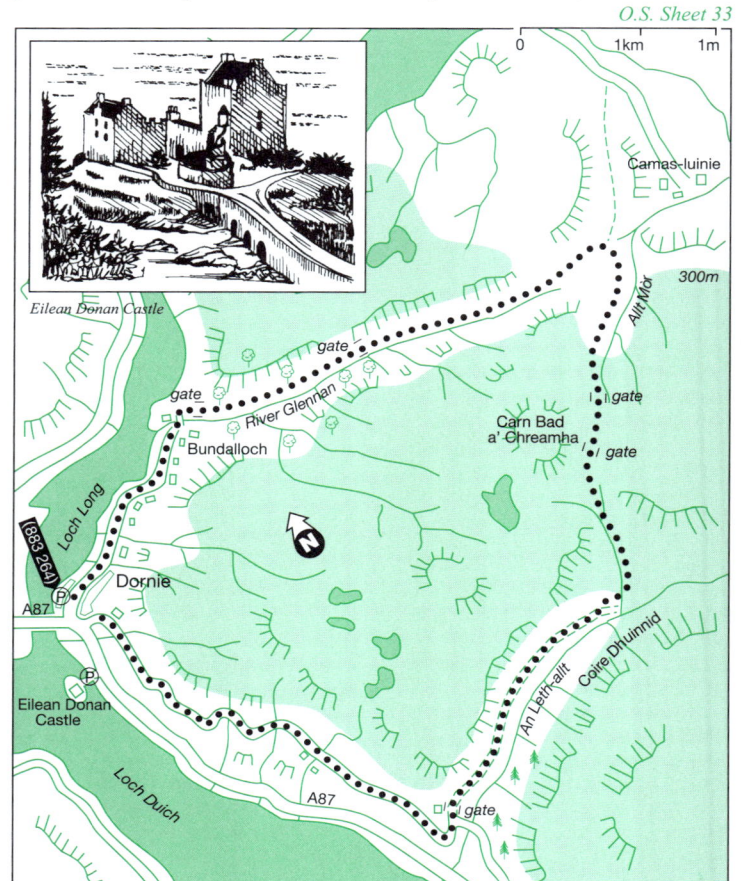

Start this walk from Dornie, at the junction of Loch Duich and Loch Long. (Eilean Donan Castle is just to the south of the village). Park in the car park in front of the Dornie Hotel and, following the signs for Bundalloch, start walking up the minor road on the east side of Loch Long.

After a little over a mile/1.6km you reach the end of the public road. Cross a wooden bridge and turn right immediately beyond, following a track up the north side of the River Glennan.

After a short distance you go through a gate and continue – now in an area where cattle are grazing. A little further on you reach a sheep fank. Beyond this, the path becomes less clear, but navigation is not difficult: just keep to the left of the burn. A little over a mile/1.6km beyond the fank the path (which is surrounded by regenerating deciduous woodland) passes through a gate in a fence. Continue up the narrowing glen – crossing the burn when necessary – to the bealach (pass) at its head. Looking back from the bealach there are (on a clear day) fine views of the Cuillins on Skye.

At this point there is no clear path. If you look at the OS map you will see a path heading just east of north from the bealach. If you have had enough climbing for the day, follow this (it is faint, but can be followed) down to the public road and turn left to return to Dornie. To continue with the main route, edge over to the right-hand side (as you have been walking) of the bealach to join a rough path climbing into the glen of Allt Mòr.

Follow this path uphill, roughly parallel to the burn down to your left. Pass through a gate in an electric fence and continue, climbing towards the watershed to the east of Carn Bad a' Chreamha.

Just short of the watershed there is a deer fence with a tall kissing-gate in it, beyond which the path continues across open moorland. The path is faint at this point; just keep to the right-hand side of the burn flowing down the slope. Looking ahead you will see the glen of a burn joining from your right. The path crosses the burn to your left just before this confluence then continues along the top of the slope above a narrow gully.

There are quad tracks crossing the slope. Ignore these and continue down the ridge above the burn – the ground is driest on this line. Ahead, you can see the broad glen of Coire Dhuinnid.

Shortly before the burn reaches the floor of the glen the path turns right, crossing it, then disappears. Drop down to the left at this point, to join a very clear track running up the glen. Turn right along this, following the northern side of An Leth-allt down the increasingly steep and narrow glen. At the foot of the glen you join a minor public road above Loch Duich.

Turn right along this road and follow it for a little more than 3 miles/5km back to Dornie, enjoying the fine views which the road's elevated position allows of Eilean Donan Castle and across Loch Duich.

28 Caisteal Grugaig — B

A short lineal route through fine coastal scenery to a ruined broch and a good viewpoint. Paths rough in places. There is a possible extension along the coast, but the path is very wet. Length: **2 miles/3km** (there and back); Height Climbed: **260ft/80m**.

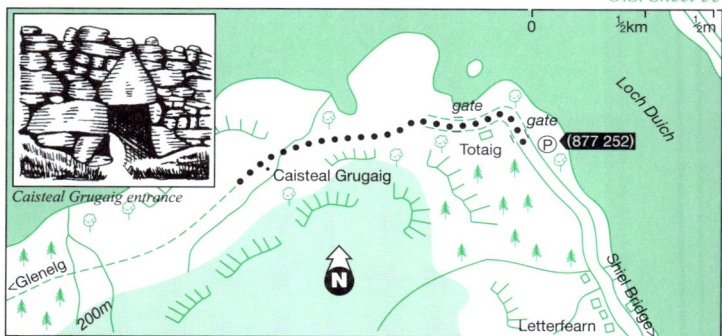

Caisteal Grugaig entrance

O.S. Sheet 33

A broch is a cylindrical Iron Age fortification. The best examples in this area are in Gleann Beag, just south of Glenelg, but Caisteal Grugaig is also well worth a visit.

To reach it, drive about 15 miles east from Kyle of Lochalsh on the A87 to reach Shiel Bridge, at the head of Loch Duich. Turn west here, onto the minor road for Glenelg and Ratagan. After a short distance there is another junction. Go right here (Ratagan, Totaig).

Follow this pleasant, narrow road along the shore of Loch Duich for a little over five miles. After passing the houses at Letterfearn the road enters woodland and climbs away from the water. Watch for a parking place amongst the trees to the right of the road.

Walk on along the road. In a short distance you reach a gate at the end of the metalled road. Continue along the track beyond, passing a white cottage by a bay (Totaig) then going through a gate in a deer fence. Beyond this the track becomes rougher.

When the path crosses a burn you will see the broch up to your left. It is in good condition – considering its age – but take great care when investigating the structure.

It is worth following the path a short way on beyond the broch. This climbs to an interpretative board, showing a reconstruction of the building. A rough path continues beyond this point, ultimately leading to Ardintoul and Glenelg (*see* Walk 29), but for this walk simply return by the same route.

29 Ardintoul — A

A fine, varied circuit, starting on clear forestry tracks and returning on rough paths by the shore and through birch woodland. Provides fine views and passes the Glenelg-Skye ferry terminus and a wide sand beach. Length: **8 miles/12.5km**; *Height Climbed:* **900ft/280m**.

O.S. Sheet 33

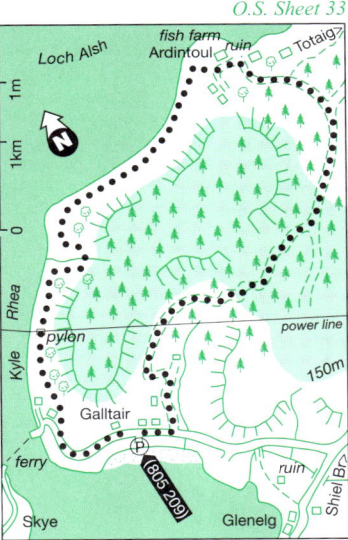

Head for the village of Glenelg (turn west on a minor road from Shiel Bridge, 15 miles south of Kyle of Lochalsh on the A87). Just before you reach the village a road heads off to your right, signposted for Galltair. Follow this for a mile to reach a parking area behind the beach to your left.

Walk back out onto the road and turn right. As you approach a rocky outcrop, a metalled entrance road heads off to your left, signposted as the path to Ardintoul Bay. Start walking up this track, with houses to your left.

When the fields to your left end, the track crosses to the left-hand side of the glen. It zig-zags up the slope then begins a steady climb through conifer woodland. There are fine views southwards down the Sound of Sleat.

The track crosses the watershed then begins its descent. There are two forked junctions (keep left at both), but otherwise the route is clear, down towards the buildings at Ardintoul.

The track becomes a beech-lined drive then reaches the shore. Go left. Ahead of you is a slipway and the burned-out remains of Ardintoul House. At a junction, go left, with the ruin of the house to your right.

After a short distance the track swings left, to pass an old steading. As it does so, turn right, off the track, and follow a grassy path down to the shore.

Turn left behind the shore, passing through a sequence of fields before the rough path climbs the slope to your left to run through birch woodland above the narrows of Kyle Rhea. Follow this undulating path through trees before exiting them behind the terminus of the Glenelg-Skye ferry.

Follow the quiet public road back to the start of the walk.

30 Sandaig _____ B

A short, lineal walk on a steep, clear path through conifers, leading to the site of Gavin Maxwell's house. Length: **3 miles/5km** (there and back); Height Climbed: **330ft/100m**.

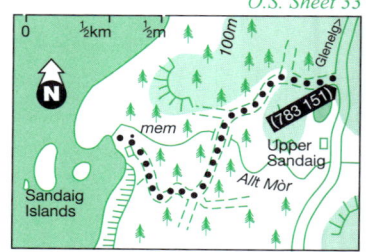

Drive south from the village of Glenelg (*see* Walk 29). After a mile, keep right at the junction at Eilanreach. After a further two miles you pass a small lochan in the conifers to the right of the road. Immediately before this a forest road heads off to the right. There is room to park near the top of this road.

At the first junction, keep left. At the second keep left again, dropping to cross the bridge over Allt Mòr. Continue to a four-way junction, where you should go right. There is one further junction beyond. Keep right again and follow the track down to the open land behind the shore.

Maxwell's house – famous from *Ring of Bright Water* – has been demolished, but there are memorials to Maxwell and Edal (the otter).

Explore the area – including the beautiful little tidal islands – and return by the same route.

31 Corran _____ B

A short, rough path along the coast – may not be possible at high water. Length: **2 miles/3km** (there and back); Height Climbed: negligible.

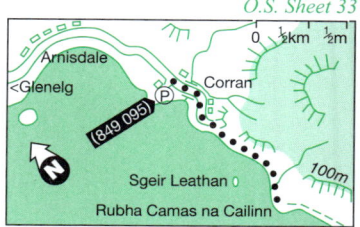

Follow the driving instructions for Walk 30, but continue for a further six miles to the little village of Corran, at the end of the road. Park by the Heritage Centre and walk on along the last part of the road; over a bridge then right, with a row of houses then sheds to your left.

You can follow the shore – now on the beach, now in the woodland above it – as far as you like (the old Right of Way runs 9 miles/14.5km to Kinloch Hourn), but it becomes difficult to follow after a mile/1.6km, so it is best to turn back from Rubha Camas na Cailinn: the little rocky headland at the end of the first big bay.